Inside Me

ADRIAN M. HURTADO

Leavitt Peak Press

ISBN: 978-1-969865-15-2 (sc)
ISBN: 978-1-969865-16-9 (e)

Rev. date: 10/02/2025

*Dedicated to those who know me
and still love me*

Inside me are so many things
Much more than I can say
If I released them all at once
I'd prob'ly float away

4

To know me, I must share some of
The things I have inside
Some I'm very free to share
And some I'd rather hide

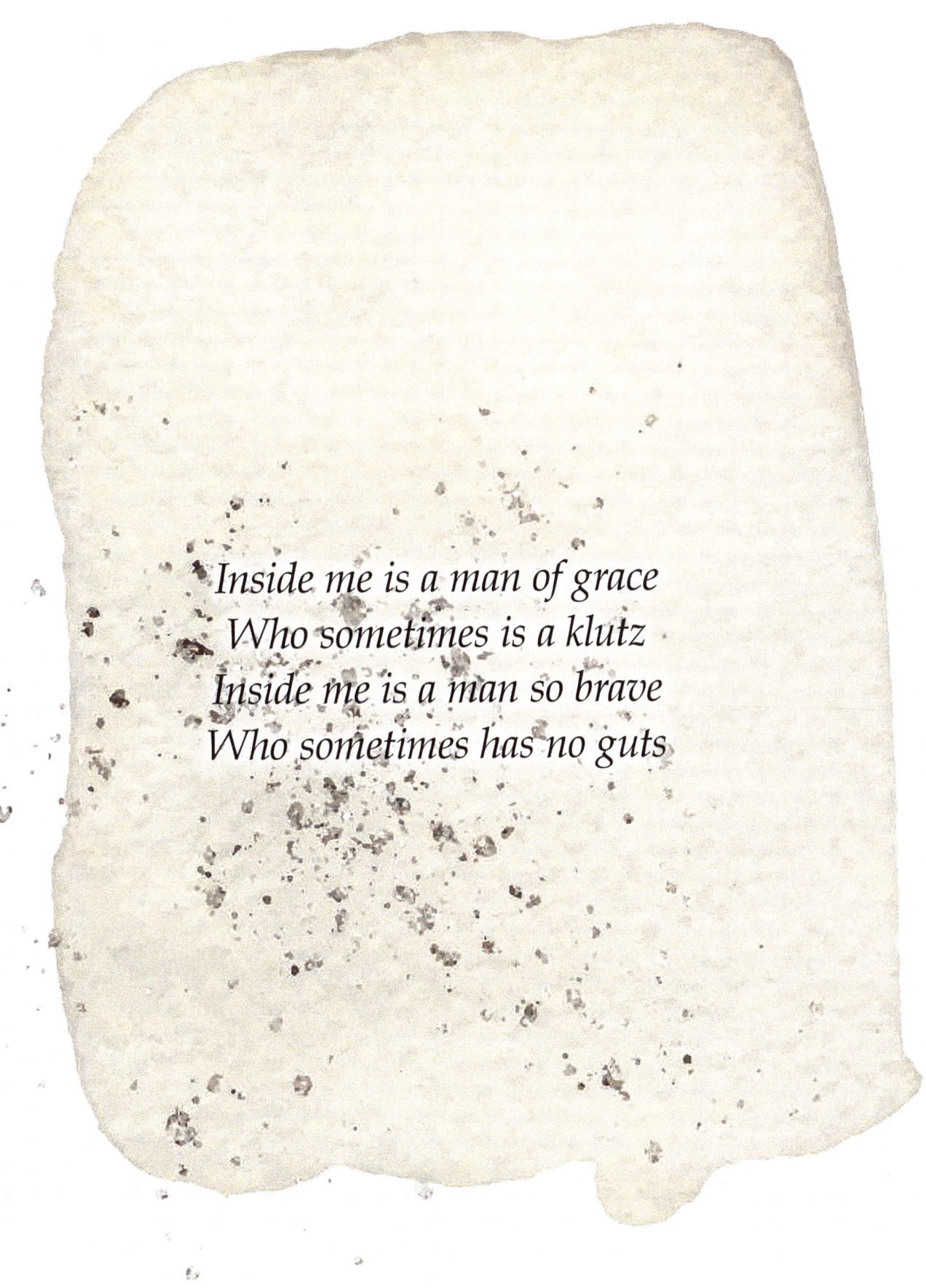

Inside me is a man of grace
Who sometimes is a klutz
Inside me is a man so brave
Who sometimes has no guts

Inside me is a man so slow
He sometimes moves too fast
A man who's happy being .first
And O.K. being last

Inside me is a man who wants
The things life has to give
Inside me is a man who'll die
But first he'll really live

Inside me is a man who's seen
The ugliness of war
Who smelled the gruesome stench of death
And learned to love life more

Inside me is a man who learns
But also wants to teach
A man who seems so far away
But not too far to reach

Inside me is a man who loves
And tries hard not to hate
Who sometimes leads a crooked life
Yet tries to keep it straight

Inside me is a man who fails
Before he can succeed
A fiercely independent man
Who reaches out in need

20

Inside me is a callous man
Who's really soft at heart
Inside me is a man who ends
By knowing how to start

Inside me is a shallow man
Whose thoughts are very deep
A straight faced, rather stoic man
Who's not ashamed to weep

Inside me is a carefree child
Who takes life day-by-day
Yet, one of quiet solitude
With nothing much to say

Inside me are a million thoughts
Just waiting to come out
As spoken words or great ideas
That show what I'm about

My life is like a reference book
That sits upon the shelf
I take me down, I look inside
And there I .find myself

AUTHOR'S PHOTO GALLERY

HARMONY, CA

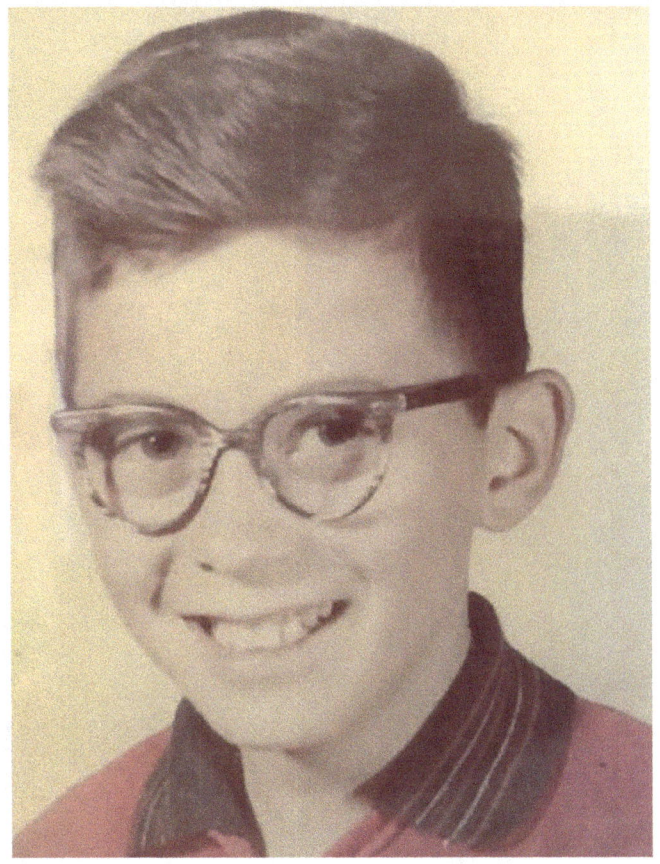